TIG WELDING
FOR BEGINNERS

Easily get good at Tig Welding

RICHARD BROOKE

Table of Contents

CHAPTER 1

What Is TIG Welding?

Tig welding

The TIG welding technique is a distinctly sophisticated, precise, and versatile arc welding technique that joins nearly all metals.

In different words, TIG welding is incredible. But, it's additionally very challenging. This article will instruct you what TIG welding is, how it works, its applications, and how to get started.

TIG, or tungsten inert gas, makes use of a non-consumable tungsten electrode to create an arc and be part of metal. It requires the use of defensive gas, most normally pure argon or argon blended with helium.

This welding method makes use of direct cutting-edge ("DC") and alternating cutting-edge ("AC") relying on the metallic to be joined.

The American Welding Society ("AWS") classifies TIG welding as "gas tungsten arc welding," however the abbreviation "GTAW" is generally used. Initially, the method used to be named "heliarc," however that time period pops up not often nowadays. You can examine greater about heliarc welding here. The special elements of TIG welding are the absence of bodily contact between the electrode and the steel portions and that the electrode is now not ate up in the process. As a result, the arc is secure and easy and produces aesthetically fascinating welds. Electrodes used in different arc welding approaches bodily engage with the steel and may additionally contain a number fluxing agents, which consequences in spatter and much less manipulate over the welding arc.

How Does TIG Welding Work?

TIG welding works with the aid of

melting the base steel with an electrical arc fashioned between the tungsten electrode and the grounded metallic (the work clamp closes the circuit).

Let's ruin it down…

Tungsten Electrode

Tungsten metallic melts at a ways greater temperatures (3422°C) than metals like metal (1371-1540°C) and aluminum (660°C). So, the tungsten electrode without problems tolerates the excessive warmness as it directs the electrical arc into the weld puddle. Plus, as the tungsten gets hotter, the electron emission improves and creates an even extra stable, easy   arc.

You can form the welding arc and cone width with the aid of grinding the tungsten electrode tip to a point. This steel is effortless to form and retains the favored configuration well. You can adjust the warmth enter and awareness through tailoring the tungsten tip shape, which is a fantastically advisable thing of TIG welding.

Filler   Metal

The TIG welding system can be part of metals with or barring filler metal. The welding arc originating from the tungsten electrode melts the two base metals and fuses them. However, to attain sturdy joints, filler steel is commonly required.

Adding filler steel is one of the difficult factors of GTAW. You ought to add the filler metallic by using dabbing a filler wire into the weld pool with one hand whilst controlling the TIG torch with the other.

Touching the tungsten with the filler metallic contaminates the electrode, requiring you to end and regrind the tungsten tip. So, including the filler metallic is problematic due to the fact the tungsten tip and the filler wire tip have to be shut and cross in the equal route besides touching.

Shielding   Gas

As the identify implies, the "tungsten inert gas" welding manner requires the usage of an inert protective fuel to defend the tungsten electrode and the molten metallic from oxidation. Inert gasses don't react with the substances used to weld. This safety is indispensable due to the fact it ensures a clean, secure surroundings for the arc and the molten steel puddle in the joint. The two most typically used defensive gasses for TIG welding are argon and helium. Argon is nearly best and receives the job executed in 99% of the cases.

However, you may also come across duties the place a helium argon mixture can enhance penetration. Just recognize it sacrifices some arc stability. Where Is TIG Welding Used? Gas tungsten arc welding is normally used for precision welds and becoming a member of unusual metals like stainless steel, aluminum, Chromoly, nickel alloys, and magnesium. However, it's additionally employed for welding everyday moderate metal if the joint first-rate need to be absolute. Otherwise, MIG welding is greater appropriate for moderate metal due to the fact it's quicker and easier.

The TIG welding manner lets in complete manipulate over the warmness enter and welding arc. Modern TIG energy sources guide pulsed TIG, and you can alter the AC balance, frequency, waveforms, and character amperage output for DCEN and DCEP parts of the AC. Plus, a foot pedal lets you reasonable amperage output in real-time as you weld.

Precise warmness manage is wished for expert skinny inventory welding, specifically with distinguished materials. For example, stainless metal retains heat, main to carbon precipitation that shortly destroys its corrosion resistance. But, if you use pulsed TIG welding, you can manipulate warmth enter and make ideal stainless metal welds.

Welding Aluminum And Magnesium

Some substances like aluminum or magnesium can solely be TIG welded if you desire to gain most joint quality. MIG welding aluminum additionally works well, however AC TIG welds are king. That's due to the fact the DCEP definitely gets rid of floor oxides whilst DCEN permits them to penetrate the material. MIG welding strength sources can't supply complete manage like TIG welders.

Tig welding ac dcep The photograph suggests how AC alternates between DCEP and DCEN and how DCEP breaks oxides whilst DCEN penetrates the metal.

You can flawlessly tailor the arc for your particular aluminum or magnesium piece by means of the use of AC stability and amplitude manage (individually enhancing DCEN and DCEP amperage output). This takes trip due to the fact you have to consider the extent of floor oxides and set the ideal AC stability and amperage output for every polarity to in shape the situation. No different arc welding technique presents so a great deal control.

Weld Looks

Finally, aesthetics play a giant position when finding out which welding system to use. Stick and flux-cored welding are now not an alternative if you choose fairly welds. While MIG welds can seem to be good, TIG welding achieves the first-class results.

tig welding stainless metal bead with argon

Imagine the use of the stick welding technique to make a

bicycle frame. It would be a catastrophe and require large post-weld cleanup.

But, on the different hand, a professional TIG welder can make the well-known "stack of dimes" bead that requires little to no cleanup. The identical goes for vehicle physique repairs, indoors furniture, or some thing else the place aesthetics are essential.

Is TIG Different Than MIG Welding?

TIG welding is very one of a kind from MIG welding due to the fact the MIG welding technique makes use of a consumable electrode that additionally acts as a filler metal.

Unlike TIG, MIG welding depends on an computerized wire feeder that pushes the filler steel wire into the molten weld pool. But, this filler wire is additionally energized, simply like the tungsten electrode in TIG welding. MIG wire is pushed from the wire feeder, via the lead, and into the MIG gun torch. Once the wire touches the metal, an arc forms, which melts the wire and base metal. So, in contrast to TIG, the electrode will become the section of the joint, and welding besides a filler steel is impossible. MIG welding additionally creates spatter due to the fact the arc extinguishes and re-ignites each and every time the wire touches the metal. This takes place many instances in a 2nd throughout a usual quick circuit MIG transfer. As a result, MIG welding inherently can't make aesthetically eye-catching welds like the TIG welding process. However, considering filler steel addition to the weld pool is automated, the MIG welding procedure is a ways simpler to learn. Plus, you can obtain a good deal greater welding velocity and enhance your productiveness in contrast to TIG welding. If you can use the MIG welding process, do so due to the fact it's extra productive. You have to use TIG welding when the joint satisfactory is paramount, when welding amazing materials, or if weld aesthetics are essential.

CHAPTER 2

What Do I Need To TIG Weld?

TIG welding gear is greater steeply-priced than MIG or stick welding gear. There are low-priced TIG welders on the market, however they don't provide all of the beforehand mentioned features for arc control.

The crucial gear for TIG welding includes:

TIG welder – the most highly-priced piece of the setup. The TIG welding laptop ought to assist AC TIG output to weld aluminum. Tungsten electrode – lanthanum, cerium, thorium, and pure tungsten rods are most often used. Thoriated tungsten is radioactive, however lanthanum is an excellent, protected substitute.

Filler rods – use ER70S-6 for normal moderate steel, ER308 for general 200 and 300-series stainless steels, and ER4043 for most aluminum applications. Shielding gasoline tank – Buy and refill, don't rent. It's less expensive that way. Read our information on protective gasoline tank sizes here, or simply get an

80CF argon fuel bottle that works amazing for most jobs and workloads.

Welding helmet – The hood have to be rated for low TIG amperage if welding skinny substances that require a low amp start. Gloves – don't use heavy-duty gloves for MIG or stick welding. Use light, bendy goatskin gloves designed for TIG. Foot pedal – it permits you to reasonable the amperage output in real-time, however no longer all welding machines aid foot pedal connection.

You additionally want to arm your self with patience. Learning how to TIG weld takes practice, a lot of time, and hands-on experience. Don't be discouraged if you fail to recreate these pristine welds posted by using famous social media welders. No one ever really masters TIG welding. We are all simply alongside for the ride. Ask any professional, and they'll all say they are nevertheless learning. But, with some practice, you'll make beautiful, steady welds in a flat, horizontal position. As you attain greater experience, you'll be capable to weld extra complicated joints and work on exclusive materials.

Pros And Cons Of TIG Welding
Advantages of GTAW:
Maximum joint quality
Welds nearly all materials
Perfect for skinny stock
Low threat of weld contamination
Weld with or barring filler metal
No spatter or smoke
It doesn't require flux or slag
Allows welding in all positions
Maximum manipulate over arc and warmness input
Provides remarkable visibility of arc and weld pool
TIG makes the best-looking welds
Disadvantages of GTAW:
It's a difficult method to learn
TIG welding is a gradual process,

which reduces productivity

Small errors in journey speed, amperage output, pulse settings, or tungsten coaching can drastically impair weld quality

Welding outside blows away the protective gas

Expensive equipment

Careers In TIG Welding

The high-quality jobs for knowledgeable TIG welders are in the aerospace and pipeline industries. However, pipeline work is regularly carried out in harsh environments. So, if you can restore airplanes, you'll have higher working conditions. Other industries consist of fabrication, structural welding, meals and beverage, and oil and gas. All of these require expert TIG operators to be part of special alloys and make complicated joints. To get a high-paid TIG welding job, you'll want to be a licensed TIG welder.

Wrapping It

TIG welding is the first-class arc welding approach for attaining high-quality, stunning welds. Thanks to a non-consumable electrode that exactly directs the arc and the severa features contemporary TIG tools offers, you can tailor the arc and warmness enter precisely as needed.

However, TIG welding is sluggish and extraordinarily tough to learn. For that reason, MIG welding is the most extensively used arc welding process. But, GTAW is the reigning king in aesthetics and cleanliness, making it irreplaceable for many welding applications. TIG welding is a secure arc welding technique that makes use of a non-consumable tungsten electrode and an inert gasoline in the welding arc to create excellent welds. It grew to become a groundbreaking success for the duration of the Nineteen Forties when it used to be first used for welding collectively aluminum and magnesium alloys in the aerospace industry.

While it commenced out as a answer to manufacture aircrafts, TIG welding finally grew to be an accelerator in one-of-a-kind industries supplying unmatched quality. A lot of developments and improvements in science have been made due to the fact that and this technique has come to be irreplaceable in many instances. Tungsten inert gasoline welding, additionally recognized as fuel tungsten arc welding (GTAW), is a welding technique that joins portions of metallic collectively via a welding current.

An inert fuel is provided to the welding torch that flows alongside the welding arc to shield the metals from oxidation and from forming small round gaps. A tungsten electrode is assembled within the welding torch, which has a greater melting factor than most metals.

TIG welding is every so often pressured with MIG welding. Although they have their similarities, there are some key variations that want to be pointed out.

Difference Between TIG and MIG

Welding

The major distinction between MIG and TIG welding method is that TIG welding makes use of a non-consumable electrode and separate filler cloth (optional). While MIG makes use of a continuous, consumable wire electrode which is robotically fed to the welding gun. TIG welding is most regularly carried out when becoming a member of pipes and skinny materials. This is thanks to its low warmness input, which preserves the microstructure of the metals. When it comes to thicker materials, MIG (metal inert gas) welding is preferred. Given its decrease price versus different welding tactics and its potential for excessive weld speeds, many hotel to the use of MIG or spot welding for mass production. TIG not often creates spatter and usually requires solely mild sprucing to cast off any discoloration. It holds an area over MIG welds when it comes to appears and hence it's desired when the workpiece is no longer covered or painted, as is regularly the case with aluminum and stainless steel. This does now not imply that MIG welds can't be aesthetically fascinating however it is as a substitute frequent for MIG welds to be painted. Depending on the project, the use of filler steel is non-obligatory for TIG welding. When feeding filler rods to the weld pool, TIG welders have to use each palms and manage the warmth enter with the pedal at the identical time. All this makes TIG welding a a long way extra difficult manner than MIG, the place the filler wire is robotically fed from the torch. Most welders commonly start out as MIG operators and then transition later into TIG welding. TIG welding is now not surely a plug-and-play process. The important distinction that units the TIG welder laptop aside from the others is its many adjustable features, such as the amperage flow, pulse amount, AC/DC output and inert gasoline flow. With all these customisable features available, the technique of TIG welding is pretty versatile. TIG Welding Process The first step in the TIG welding manner is to regulate the laptop to the right settings, such as the cutting-edge and voltage, via the rotating knobs on the machine. Next, the right stress for the inert fuel in the grant tank have to be set thru a flowmeter regulator. The

TIG torch need to additionally be modified in accordance to the mission necessities with the aid of selecting an electrode with the right diameter, TIG collet, and different parts. Above the entirety else, prioritise having smooth defensive tools to have clear imaginative and prescient whilst doing welds.

After all the prep work is done, it's time to weld the metals together. Several matters have to be regarded to make certain a clean float of operation: the arc length, journey speed, torch angle, and different precautionary measures. TIG welds can run weld beads except filler material, solely melting the base metals, however you can use it with filler rods or steel coils if the task requires it to. Although the web is stuffed with so-called TIG bloodless welding movies and pictures, this approach has nothing to do with the proper bloodless welding process. It focuses on the look of the welds however it clearly lacks fusion due to drastically decreased warmth enter and is alternatively ineffective in growing strong, everlasting joints.

Important Details While Working

A acceptable ahead attitude is crucial when the use of the torch to stop air pocket buildup that creates porosity in the bead. A quick arc size need to be maintained for most excellent control. The electric powered arc will widen as the arc size is increased.

Consistent journey velocity is the key to retaining a steady bead. Increasing the pace will purpose a narrowing of the weld bead. Avoid touching the weld pool with the tungsten electrode. The dimension of the filler metallic need to be right and the manner of feeding it to the weld should be done with acceptable control.

The form of the tungsten electrode's tip need to usually be consistent. It can be sharpened on a grinding wheel.

CHAPTER 3

Materials in Gas Tungsten Arc Welding

TIG welders can utilise an array of materials. Some of the base substances listed for tungsten inert fuel arc welding are:

Aluminium

Brass

Bronze

Carbon   steel

Copper

Gold

Magnesium

Mild   Steel

Nickel

Stainless   steel

Titanium   steel

Different   alloys

You want to maintain in thinking that the procedure of TIG welding for every cloth is barely different. Modifications can vary from the measurement of the electrode diameter down to the electric powered arc applied in the materials. It is essential that the electrode has the correct diameter and that the amperage utilized is correct. The decrease the current, the smaller the tip perspective and the diameter of the electrode.

Non-Consumable Tungsten Electrode

TIG welding tungsten electrodes Tungsten is used in this system seeing that this rare, steel issue intrinsically has a excessive melting temperature (3422°C) when in contrast to different metals (e.g. stainless metal has a melting factor from 1400 to 1530°C). Tungsten gives first-rate electrical conductivity except being consumed. Though, erosion can nonetheless take place on the tip throughout the shielded steel arc welding procedure. Tungsten electrodes can additionally be alloyed to enhance their houses relying on the weld type. Here are some frequent examples:

Pure tungsten electrode (green) – They provide suitable arc balance when the use of AC current. Used for mild metals considering the fact that they hold a clean, balled end. These are additionally the most inexpensive and utilized for typical reason work.

Thoriated electrodes (1% thorium

yellow; 2% red; 3% purple) – Quite frequent in the welding scene as they had been the first to beat pure tungsten electrodes in DC welding arc performance.

They have a excessive cutting-edge carrying capability and they preserve the form of the tip longer. However, thorium emits alpha radiation, which can damage the respiratory system. A dirt extraction machine is required for amassing the dirt at some point of tip grinding.

Lanthaned electrodes (1% lanthanium black, 1.5% gold, 2% blue) – Non-radioactive electrode alloyed with lanthanum oxide.

Characterised via superb arc steadiness homes with low erosion rate. A bit much less environment friendly than thoriated electrodes. Ceriated electrodes (2% cerium grey) – Non-radioactive electrode alloyed with cerium oxide. These electrodes have top notch arc beginning however much less modern-day capability than lanthaned electrodes. Zirconiated electrodes (0.7-0.9% zirconium white, 0.15-0.5% brown) – These electrodes mix tungsten with zirconium oxide. This alloy has a excessive resistance to infection and longer electrode life. Produces an extraordinarily secure arc, therefore it is used when the very best excellent is needed. Cerium lanthanium electrodes (pink) – A mixture of ceriated and lanthaned electrodes imparting simplified arc ignition with a lengthy lifestyles span.

Inert Gas

Inert protecting gasoline is fed to the TIG torch to hold the weld pool free from illness whilst the modern is provided to the welding arc. The protecting gasoline float is integral in defending the weld puddle from oxidation and impurities from the environment whilst the metals are melted and fused alongside with the filler rod. The most frequent protecting gasoline used for this technique is argon. Other combos of hydrogen and argon and a combination of helium and argon are used when other elements are regarded (e.g. metals to be welded, welding speed, cloth penetration etc).

Welding Torch

TIG welding gun

A welding torch is a mechanical device specialised in melting and fusing metals. It has countless kinds relying on its use: Air-cooled TIG torches solely have one fuel input and are greater susceptible to overheating, in contrast to water-cooled TIG torches. The main use of these torches is for thin-walled metals and minor projects. Water-cooled TIG torches have a fuel enter whilst having an enter and output for water lines. This is an gain for large initiatives that want fast cooling. This comes with its rate though, as a water cooler device has to be installed. Power Source The source of the modern in fuel tungsten arc welding must be drooping and constant. This lets in for secure and regular warmth input. You can additionally swap between alternating contemporary

(AC) to direct modern-day (DC) electricity supply relying on the fabric kind and weld output you desire.

AC vs DC power

There are three alternatives accessible for the welding contemporary alongside with its personal respective uses:

AC welding makes use of an alternating modern-day between the high-quality and poor polarities, keeping the warmness barring overheating the base material. Commonly used substances are aluminium and magnesium.

DC electricity electrode poor

makes use of the poor polarity on the torch to pinpoint the power glide to the material, a good deal like a hose spraying water on a centered area. This makes it extra attractive to all metals, apart from aluminium and magnesium. DC strength electrode high-quality is hardly ever used in TIG welding in view that the modern is flowing in the direction of the electrode, making it ball up from the fast warmth input. The solely plus facet in DCEP is the presence of a "cleaning action" whereby the oxides in the weld pool's floor provide off a bright appearance. Another element to preserve in thought is the utilized frequency Hz. Lower frequencies create a wider bead with first rate penetration, whereas greater frequencies enable for extra manipulate and penetration in the weld area.

CHAPTER 4

Advantages of TIG Welding

TIG welding can be carried out on a vast array of unique metals and alloys.

A TIG welder has many customisable functions, best for particular operations. Applicable to various sorts of steel thicknesses and complicated metallic welding. Although for in reality thick metals, MIG or stick welding is preferred. A non-consumable electrode and a steady arc permit for increased manage and create splendid TIG welds.

Safe gases are used in this fuel steel arc welding process, as a end result it has fewer weld defects. TIG welding can be carried out at awkward angles. An instance would be its utility in welding overhangs, the place the welding torch has to be in a special position.

It is handy to view the work piece seeing that the protective gasoline is colourless with minimal smoke formed.

Disadvantages of TIG Welding

TIG welding requires a lot of ability from the operator. Welding time is notably longer in contrast to different welding techniques.

Using the incorrect polarity can effortlessly contaminate the weld bead.

The typical weld power diminishes when exhibiting a lack of manage over the warmness input. This additionally negatively influences the microstructure of the metals. Without a managed environment, primarily a wind-free environment, it would possibly be hard to preserve a consistent fuel float over the weld area. Compared to different welding techniques, the tools and inert gases are extra pricey. Important Points To Remember TIG welding presents correct and handsome weld beads with properly penetration. It is the favored approach for welding aluminum and magnesium alloys, alongside with many different metals consisting of stainless steel. It is a bit extra luxurious and slower technique when in contrast to some different kinds of welding however it is irreplaceable when growing greater pleasant welds.

Its consistency and versatility enable it to be particularly alluring throughout nearly all industries, from gurus to hobbyists alike. Although TIG technique can be computerized with the use of welding robots, the guide welding technique nonetheless has pretty a steep studying curve and to acquire the great results, it is most regularly carried out with the aid of skilled welders.

www.ingramcontent.com/pod-product-compliance
Lightning Source LLC
Chambersburg PA
CBHW070324160726
47999CB00003B/1139